INFOMOJIS

SPORTS

First published in Great Britain
in 2019 by Wayland
Copyright © Hodder and Stoughton, 2019
All rights reserved

Editor: Amy Pimperton
Produced by Tall Tree Ltd
Editor: Jon Richards
Designer: Ed Simkins

ISBN: 978 1 5263 0705 7

Wayland
An imprint of Hachette Children's Group
Part of Hodder and Stoughton
Carmelite House
50 Victoria Embankment
London EC4Y 0DZ

An Hachette UK Company
www.hachette.co.uk
www.hachettechildrens.co.uk

Printed and bound in China

The facts and figures provided within this
book are believed to be correct at the time
of printing.

MIX
Paper from
responsible sources
FSC® C104740

This book uses different units to measure different things:
Distance is measured using yards, centimetres (cm), metres (m), kilometres (km)
and miles.
Speed is measured using kilometres per hour (kph).
Mass is measured using kilogrammes (kg).
Sound level is measured using decibels (dB).

FOOTBALL CRAZY

Every week, millions of people around the world take part in or watch a whole host of sports. The biggest of these sports is football, and it comes in many forms, whether it's American football, association football (or 'soccer' as some people call it), Gaelic football, Aussie Rules football or rugby football. They all have their roots in various ancient ball games, as well as a violent game called mob football.

Q: When did people start playing football?

A: Evidence of early ball games dates back thousands of years.

FOOTBALL ROOTS

5000 BCE – an ancient ball game called *cuju* or *ts'u chu* was played in China. It involved a group of players standing in a circle passing a ball between them and trying to stop it from hitting the ground.

1000 BCE – *Kemari* was played in Japan using a ball stuffed with sawdust.

400 BCE – the ancient Greeks played a ball game called *episkyros*.

CE 700 – the earliest accounts of mob football played in England.

A violent game
Mob football involved two large teams who used any means possible to move a ball towards an opponents 'goal', which could have been a simple post. Games were usually violent and injuries common. It was so disruptive that, on 13 April 1314, the English monarch, King Edward II (1284–1327) issued a proclamation banning the sport. The ban remained in place for nearly 300 years.

KING EDWARD II

Many forms of football

During the 1800s, teams in countries around the world joined together to form their own organisations and create their own forms, or codes, of football.

Football (association football or soccer) – The laws for this code were written in 1863 and the first Football Association was formed in England. The game is played by two teams of 11 players (plus substitutes).

Rugby football – Unhappy with the creation of association football laws, some clubs decided to formalise their own code of the sport, creating rugby football in 1871. Today, two separate codes of rugby exists. Rugby union is played by two teams of 15 players, while rugby league is played by two teams of 13 players.

Gaelic football – The first Gaelic football rules were drawn up in February 1887 to help promote and preserve traditional Irish sports. The game is played by two teams of 15 players each.

Aussie Rules – The first Australian Rules football matches were played in 1858. This sport is played by two teams with 18 players each.

American football – The first American football, or gridiron, game was played in November 1869. It involves two teams with 11 players on the pitch, or 'field', for each side at any one time.

TRACK AND FIELD

Whether it's running, jumping or throwing, track and field athletes are continuously pushing themselves to run faster, jump higher, and throw farther than ever before.

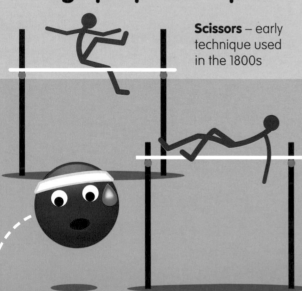

High jump techniques

Scissors – early technique used in the 1800s

Eastern and western roll – introduced in early 1900s, raising world record to more than 2 m

Straddle – introduced in 1930s and 1940s, pushing the record up to 2.28 m

Fosbury Flop – first used by American athlete Dick Fosbury to win the 1968 Olympics and now used by all high-jumpers

FASTER, HIGHER, STRONGER

Here's how athletes have improved since the early days of the modern Olympics.

RESULTS FROM 1896 ATHENS OLYMPICS
(all competitors were men)

100 metres Thomas Burke (USA)
12.0 seconds

400 metres Thomas Burke (USA)
54.2 seconds

1,500 metres Edwin Flack (Australia)
4 minutes 33.2 seconds

Marathon Spyridon Louis (Greece)
2 hours 58 minutes 50 seconds

High jump Ellery Clark (USA)
1.81 m

Long jump Ellery Clark (USA)
6.35 m

Discus throw Robert Garrett (USA)
29.15 m

The Summer Olympic Games is a multi-sport event held every four years. It sees thousands of athletes compete in a wide range of sports, not just track-and-field athletics.

RESULTS FROM 2016 RIO DE JANEIRO OLYMPICS
(men's results first)

100 metres Usain Bolt (Jamaica) 9.81 seconds, Elaine Thompson (Jamaica) 10.71 seconds

400 metres Wayde van Niekerk (South Africa) 43.04 seconds, Shaunae Miller (Bahamas) 49.44 seconds

1,500 metres Matthew Centrowitz, Jr. (USA) 3 minutes 50.0 seconds, Faith Kipyegon (Kenya) 4 minutes 8.92 seconds

Marathon Eliud Kipchoge (Kenya) 2 hours 8 minutes 44 seconds, Jemima Sumgong (Kenya) 2 hours 24 minutes 4 seconds

High jump Derek Drouin (Canada) 2.38 m, Ruth Beitia (Spain) 1.97 m

Long jump Jeff Henderson (USA) 8.38 m, Tianna Bartoletta (USA) 7.17 m

Discus throw Christoph Harting (Germany) 68.37 m, Sandra Perković (Croatia) 69.21 m

Q: Who are the fastest runners in the world?

A: My name is Florence Griffith-Joyner and I ran the fastest ever women's 100 m in 10.49 seconds in 1988. The fastest man in the world is Usain Bolt who ran the 100 m in 9.58 seconds in 2009.

FLORENCE GRIFFITH-JOYNER

Q: What was unusual about Olympic sprinter Thomas Burke (1875–1929)?

A: He used a crouch start, with one knee on the ground, which was uncommon at the time – runners usually used a standing start. Today, all sprinters use a crouching start.

BATS, STICKS AND BALLS

Requiring power, pace and accuracy, these sports are guaranteed to test the abilities of the most talented sports men and women.

CRICKET

I hold the record for the fastest delivery in a cricket match. While playing for Pakistan against England in 2003, I bowled at 161.3 kph.

SHOAIB AKHTAR

West Indies batsman, Brian Lara, holds the record for the highest individual score in a test match when he scored 400 not out against England. The highest test score by a woman was 242. It was achieved by Pakistan's Kiran Baluch against the West Indies in 2004.

Shinty is a team game, similar to hockey, and which is played with sticks and a ball. Thousands of years ago, early shinty balls were made from sheep vertebrae (backbones) and even cow dung!

BASEBALL

I hold the record for the fastest baseball pitch of 169.1 kph while playing against the San Diego Pirates in 2010.

AROLDIS CHAPMAN

In 1987, Joey Meyer of the Denver Zephyrs hit the longest confirmed home run in professional baseball, when he smashed the ball for 177 m.

GOLF

Q: How far can you hit a golf ball?

A: In 1974, Mike Austin hit a golf ball for 515 yards (470 m) while playing in Las Vegas, Nevada, USA. His drive (first shot) actually flew 65 yards past the hole!

On 6 February 1971, astronaut Alan Shepard (1923–1998) actually played golf on the Moon! He hit two golf balls, one of which managed to travel for more than 200 yards.

RACKET SPORTS

All you have to do is use a racket to hit a ball or a shuttlecock around a court. Sounds simple, but with the speeds these sports can reach it's enough to test the hand-eye coordination of even the most talented athletes.

Tennis points

Tennis scoring may have come from a clock face. As a player scored a point, the hand was moved around 15 minutes (so 15, 30). However, as a player must win a game by two clear points, they used 40, instead of 45. If both players are on 40 ('deuce'), the hand would move on another 10 minutes ('advantage'), before then moving up to 60 ('game').

Game

Advantage

15

40
(Deuce)

30

The name for zero points 'love' may also come from the French words l'oeuf meaning 'the egg', because zeros look a little like eggs when written down.

After dinner

Table tennis started as an after-dinner game – the table was cleared, books were stood on end as a net, and two more books were used as bats to hit a golf ball between players. Lighter celluloid balls were introduced in 1901.

Squashy, squashier, squashiest

Squash is played using a squashy rubber ball. The balls vary in squishiness, with softer, slower balls used by better players. They are graded using coloured dots. Good squash players use slower balls, because they bounce lower and are harder to hit.

Blue:
fast
very high bounce
beginners

Red:
medium
high bounce
average players

Double yellow:
very slow
very low bounce
very good players

Yellow:
slow
low bounce
good players

HOW FAST?

Table tennis – fastest hit – 116 kph by Łukasz Budner (Poland)

Squash – fastest hit – 281.6 kph by Cameron Pilley (Australia)

Badminton – fastest smash – 493 kph by Tan Boon Hoeng (Malaysia)

Tennis – fastest serve – 263 kph by Samuel Groth (Australia)

Badminton

In the early days, badminton was played using either rubber-and-feather shuttlecocks or with woollen balls in wet or windy weather.

TARGET SPORTS

A steady hand and a keen eye are needed for these sports, where the aim is to guide an arrow or ball to the centre of a target.

Bullseye!
An archery target is divided into rings, with each ring scoring a different number of points – the closer to the centre of the target, known as the bullseye, the greater the score.

10 9 8 7 6 5 4 3 2 1

Q: How far can you accurately shoot a bow and arrow?

A: The longest accurate distance in archery was achieved by Matt Stutzman of the USA. In 2015, he hit a target that was positioned 283.47 metres away – nearly the length of three football pitches! Matt was born without arms and the Paralympian uses his foot and chin to draw back and release his bow.

MATT STUTZMAN

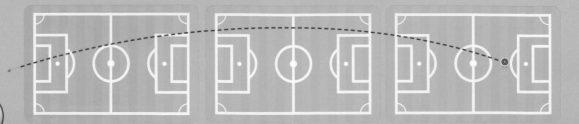

Darts

The longest marathon for a singles darts match was set in March 2014 by Wayne Mitchell and Mark Dye of the UK. They played for an astonishing 50 hours, 50 minutes and 50 seconds. At one point, Wayne had to start throwing with his left hand, because his right hand hurt so much. OUCH!!!!

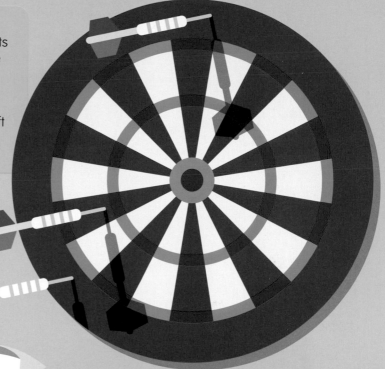

TABLE TOP

Cue sports

Table top sports involving balls being hit into each other and into pockets by using a cue, developed from outdoor target sports, such as bowls and croquet. King Louis XI of France (1423–1483) had the first known indoor billiard table. Over the years, three main cue sports evolved – pool, snooker and billiards, each using different numbers and arrangements of balls.

Pool

Snooker

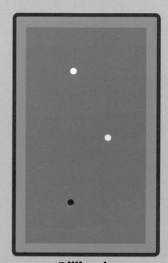

Billiards

Q: How many balls are there in eight-ball pool?

A: 16! each player uses the white cue ball and must pot any balls to win – either all their own coloured balls ('spots' or 'stripes') plus the black, the eight-ball.

WINTER SPORTS

Snowy and cold weather doesn't have to stop play – these sports need ice and snow to happen, whether it's smashing a puck across a rink, leaping as far as you can in a ski jump or racing down a run in a bobsleigh.

ICE HOCKEY FACTS

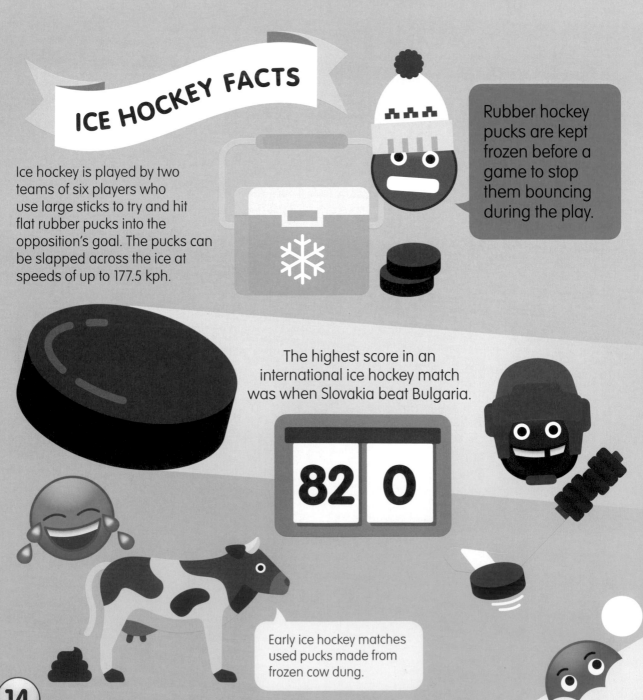

Ice hockey is played by two teams of six players who use large sticks to try and hit flat rubber pucks into the opposition's goal. The pucks can be slapped across the ice at speeds of up to 177.5 kph.

Rubber hockey pucks are kept frozen before a game to stop them bouncing during the play.

The highest score in an international ice hockey match was when Slovakia beat Bulgaria.

82 | 0

Early ice hockey matches used pucks made from frozen cow dung.

BOBSLEIGH, SKELETON AND LUGE

Skeleton sees one person steering a small sled down a frozen track riding face down.

Bobsleigh involves teams of two or four pushing and riding a bobsleigh down a track containing twists, turns and banked corners.

Luge sees one or two people sliding down the track face up.

In all three sliding sports, competitors reach speeds of about 140 kph.

In 2017, Stefan Kraft from Austria set a new record for the longest-ever ski jump, with a distance of 253.5 m, which is longer than the Golden Gate Bridge, San Francisco, USA, (227 m).

THAT'S SNOW BUSINESS!

Karine Ruby (1978–2009) is one of the most decorated snowboarders, ever. She won two Olympic medals and 10 medals at the FIS World Championships.

KARINE RUBY

King of speed – the fastest person on skis is Italian Ivan Origone, who set a speed of 254.958 kph in March 2016.

DIVING AND SWIMMING

Whether it's splashing about in a pool, or plunging from the highest diving board, these water sports involve feats of skill and endurance – just remember to take a deep breath!

SWIMMING

Q: Who's the fastest swimmer in the world?

A: César Cielo of Brazil swam the 50-m freestyle in 20.91 seconds to set a World Record. That's the same as swimming 1 km in 418.2 seconds (6 minutes 58.2 seconds) or 8.6 kph.

CÉSAR CIELO

Q: How many different strokes are used in competitive swimming?

A: There are four main strokes:
• front crawl
• breaststroke
• backstroke
• butterfly.

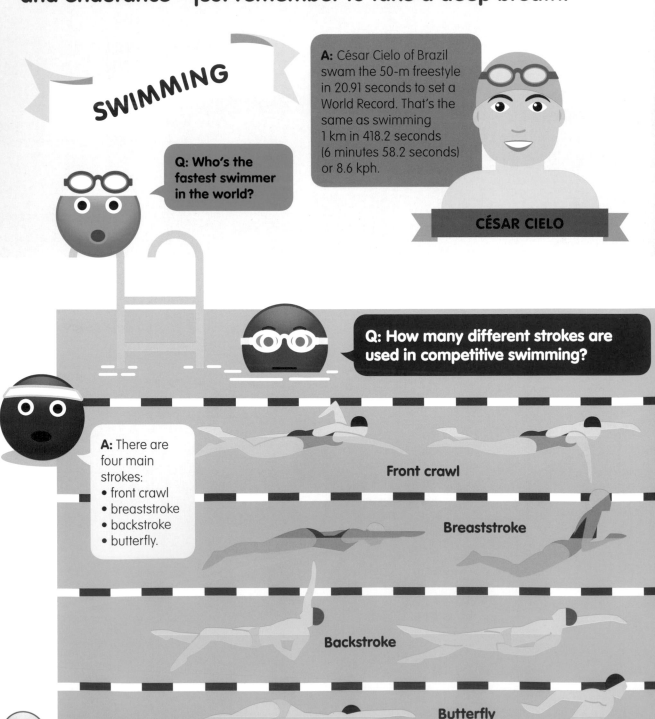

Front crawl

Breaststroke

Backstroke

Butterfly

Extreme swimming

In May 2012, Irish swimmer Steve Redmond became the first person to swim the Ocean's Seven. These are:

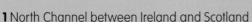

1 North Channel between Ireland and Scotland

2 Cook Strait between North Island and South Island in New Zealand

3 Moloka'i Channel between the islands of O'ahu and Moloka'i, Hawaii, USA

4 English Channel between England and France

5 Catalina Channel between Santa Catalina Island and Southern California, USA

6 Tsugaru Strait between Honshu and Hokkaido, Japan

7 Strait of Gibraltar between Africa and Europe

Freediving involves seeing how far or how deep a diver can swim underwater on a single breath.

Mateusz Malina (Poland) and Giorgos Panagiotakis (Greece) both hold the record distance of 300 m for swimming as far as possible while using fins. They set the record on the same day!

No-limits freediving, sees divers use a weighted sled to dive down. They then use an inflatable bag to rise to the surface. The record depth was set by Herbert Nitsch of Austria who descended to a depth of 214 m.

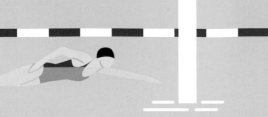

High diving

On 4 August 2015, Lazaro Schaller of Switzerland set a world record for a high dive from a diving board of 58.8 m.

COMBAT SPORTS

If you like your pastimes with a little more aggression, then these could be the sports for you – just make sure you're wearing the right protective clothing!

IN THE RING

Modern professional boxing matches are divided into rounds lasting 3 minutes and there can be up to 12 rounds in a match.

In contrast, a match in 1867 between Jack Jones and Patsy Tunney in Cheshire, UK, lasted for 4 hours 30 minutes and contained 276 rounds, before Jones won the fight.

En garde!
Fencing uses three different types of sword. Competitors use the sword to strike different body parts in order to score points.

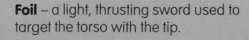

Foil – a light, thrusting sword used to target the torso with the tip.

Épée – a thrusting sword that's heavier than a foil and can score on any part of an opponent's body, as long as it's with the tip of the blade.

Sabre – used for cutting and thrusting and can score points on arms, upper body and head using the side of the blade and the tip.

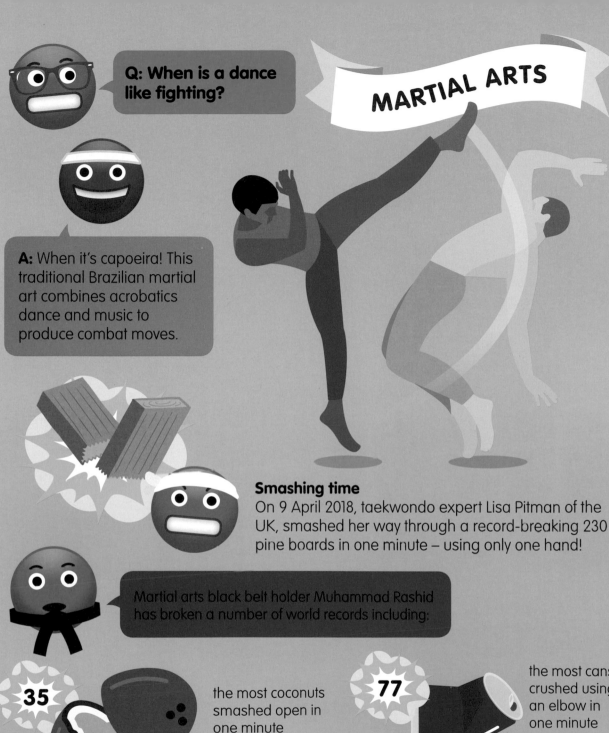

Q: When is a dance like fighting?

MARTIAL ARTS

A: When it's capoeira! This traditional Brazilian martial art combines acrobatics dance and music to produce combat moves.

Smashing time
On 9 April 2018, taekwondo expert Lisa Pitman of the UK, smashed her way through a record-breaking 230 pine boards in one minute – using only one hand!

Martial arts black belt holder Muhammad Rashid has broken a number of world records including:

35 the most coconuts smashed open in one minute

the most watermelons crushed with the head in one minute

77 the most cans crushed using an elbow in one minute

49

the most nunchaku hits in one minute

350

DO NOT TRY THIS AT HOME!

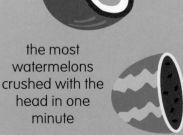

EXTREME SPORTS

These sports are not for the faint-hearted, but they do provide plenty of thrills and spills for anyone wanting to skim over waves, fly through the air or zoom down a mountainside.

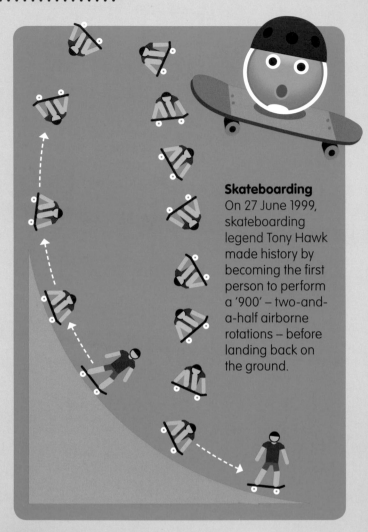

Skateboarding
On 27 June 1999, skateboarding legend Tony Hawk made history by becoming the first person to perform a '900' – two-and-a-half airborne rotations – before landing back on the ground.

Surfing
Rodrigo Koxa of Brazil holds the world record for the tallest wave ever surfed. He rode a giant 24.4-m monster off the coast of Portugal in 2017.

Water skiing
On 1 July 2017, Canadian waterskier Ryan Dodd set a world record for the longest waterski jump covering a distance of 77.4 m …

… that's longer than the wingspan of a 747 Jumbo Jet (68.5 m).

In May 2013, stuntman Gary Connery jumped out of a helicopter from a height of 730 metres and landed safely on the ground – WITHOUT USING A PARACHUTE!! He used a wingsuit to slow his fall and bring him safely in to land.

Wingsuit
Wingsuits are specially designed outfits with wings fitted under each arm and between the legs, allowing the wearer to glide through the air.

Q: What's the fastest speed a wingsuit wearer has flown?

A: In May 2017, Fraser Corsan (UK) reached 396.86 kph while wearing a wingsuit.

GRAVEL

SNOW

Mountain biking
Frenchman Éric Barone holds the world speed records for cycling on gravel and on snow. Using a custom-made prototype bike, he hit 172 kph on gravel, but went even faster on snow, reaching a speed of 227.720 kph in March 2017.

MOTOR SPORTS

People have been racing cars, motorbikes, boats and planes from the moment they were invented, pushing their speeds and the technology behind them to the limits – and beyond – in a quest to go faster and faster.

STRAIGHT LINE SPEED

Drag racing involves blasting along a straight track, usually a quarter of a mile (about 400 m) long.

The fastest dragsters can reach speeds of more than 540 kph, completing the race in less than 3.7 seconds.

Many dragsters have a wheelie bar fitted to the back to stop them from flipping over when they accelerate away.

WATER MOTOR SPORTS

Powerboating was invented by Frenchman Jean Lenoir (1822–1900), who first fitted a petrol engine to a boat in 1861.

FLYING SPORTS

Air racing sees pilots flying around a course to record the quickest time or the most points.

Open-wheel racing cars have the wheels sticking out of the sides of their bodies. They include Formula One cars and Indy Cars.

Track days
Racing cars come in many different shapes.

Other types of racing cars include sports cars, touring cars and stock cars.

Powerboating was an event at the 1908 London Olympics, the only time motor sports appeared at the Games.

Inshore powerboat racing involves competitors powering around a course laid out on a lake, river, dock or sheltered bay, with boats reaching 250 kph. Offshore powerboat racing sees ocean-going powerboats racing across the open sea at speeds of more than 250 kph.

TOURNAMENTS

Today's sporting tournaments are watched by billions of people and feature the best athletes competing for huge prizes – a far cry from the earliest sporting competitions, where the winning prize could be a twig!

These tournaments are some of the most-watched on the planet:

- **Women's Football World Cup** – 750 million viewers over the entire tournament
- **Tour de France** – 1.5 billion viewers throughout the event
- **Summer Olympics** – 3.5 billion viewers
- **Cricket World Cup** – more than 1 billion viewers for the final
- **FIFA World Cup** – average of 200 million viewers per game with the final watched by more than 900 million
- **UEFA Champions League** – 350 million watch the final
- **Super Bowl** – more than 110 million viewers

OLYMPICS

Held every four years, the modern Summer Olympic Games see thousands of athletes from more than 200 nations compete in a wide range of sports.

The winner of the first Olympic running, or stadion, race was Coroebus, a cook from Elis, ancient Greece, who's prize was an olive branch.

The original Olympic Games was held in honour of the Greek god Zeus at Olympia, Greece. First held in 776 BCE, the tournament featured athletic competitions, as well as wrestling, and horse and chariot races.

WORLD CUP

The first football World Cup took place in 1930. Teams from 13 countries travelled to Uruguay, where the hosts won the tournament.

The 2018 World Cup in Russia was contested by 32 teams, with France beating Croatia in the final to win the tournament.

The UEFA Champions League is one of the richest sports competitions in the world, with a total prize pool of around US$1.5 billion paid out to teams taking part.

A 30-second advert during Super Bowl I in 1967 cost US$37,500 to show on TV. In 2018, a 30-second advert shown during Super Bowl LII (52) cost more than US$5 million to air on TV.

EYES ON THE PRIZE

Athletes and sports men and women take part in competitions to win. And the winners are awarded medals, cups, trophies and even jerseys and jackets to show that they are the best on the pitch, field, course, court or track.

Q: Who is the most successful Olympian of all time?

A: American swimmer Michael Phelps won 28 medals (23 gold, 3 silver and 2 bronze) in an Olympic career spanning four Olympic Games from 2004–2016.

MICHAEL PHELPS

The woman who won the most Olympic medals is gymnast Larisa Latynina from the former Soviet Union. She won 18 medals, including 9 golds, 5 silvers and 4 bronzes between 1956 and 1964.

Leaders in cycling's Tour de France wear different coloured jerseys to show which class they are leading in.

The best cyclist in the mountain stages is called 'The King of the Mountains' and wears a spotted jersey.

The best young rider (under the age of 26) wears a white jersey.

The race leader wears a yellow jersey.

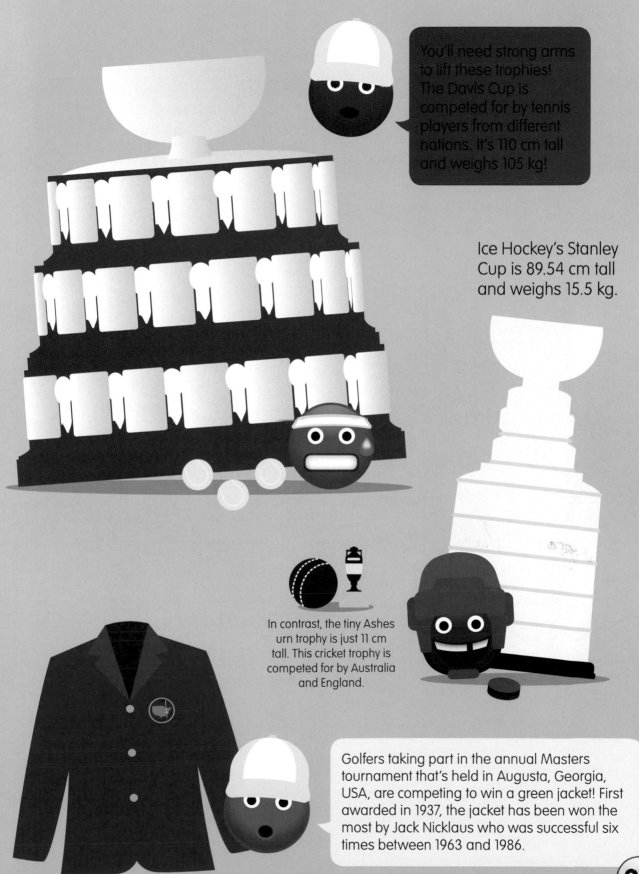

You'll need strong arms to lift these trophies! The Davis Cup is competed for by tennis players from different nations. It's 110 cm tall and weighs 105 kg!

Ice Hockey's Stanley Cup is 89.54 cm tall and weighs 15.5 kg.

In contrast, the tiny Ashes urn trophy is just 11 cm tall. This cricket trophy is competed for by Australia and England.

Golfers taking part in the annual Masters tournament that's held in Augusta, Georgia, USA, are competing to win a green jacket! First awarded in 1937, the jacket has been won the most by Jack Nicklaus who was successful six times between 1963 and 1986.

FANS AND VENUES

The biggest and best sporting events need the biggest and best sporting venues. And these stadiums play host to the most popular, loudest and even earthquake-rivalling competitions on the planet.

Q: Where would you find the world's biggest team sports stadium?

A: In the North Korean capital of Pyongyang. The Rungrado May Day Stadium has a seating capacity of 150,000 and is used to stage football matches, wrestling events and Communist party rallies.

The huge Circus Maximus in ancient Rome could hold up to 250,000 people to watch chariot races around the oval-shaped track.

I keep going round in circles!

The modern equivalent of the Circus Maximus is the Indianapolis Motor Speedway. It has seating for 257,325 people but, with standing spectators, it can hold up to 400,000 fans.

The sporting event with possibly the biggest spectator crowd is the Tour de France. Held over a little more than three weeks, up to 15 million people line the route of the stages to watch the cyclists race by.

Ear splitting

According to Guinness World Records, the loudest roar made by a sports crowd took place at Arrowhead Stadium, Kansas City, USA, when fans of the American football team, the Kansas City Chiefs, shouted to 142.2 dB in 2014. In comparison, a military jet taking off makes only 130 dB.

Seattle

USA Kansas

Fans of another American football team, the Seattle Seahawks, celebrate so loudly that they have set off earthquake meters in the nearby University of Washington.

GLOSSARY

BATSMAN
A male or female player, usually in cricket, that is responsible for batting the ball.

BOBSLEIGH
A vehicle that runs on thin metal blades and is used to race downhill along U-shaped tracks made of ice. Bobsleighs are usually crewed by two or four people.

BOWLS
A game similar to bowling where players bowl a ball as close as possible to a previously bowled ball, called the 'jack'.

BULLSEYE
The name given to the innermost ring or circle of an archery target or dartboard.

CELLULOID
A lightweight plastic material that is used to make table tennis balls.

CODE
Used to refer to different forms of the same sport. For example, rugby union and rugby league are two codes of rugby football.

CROQUET
A game played on grass where each player hits a wooden ball through a series of square-topped hoops using a mallet (long-handled stick).

CROUCHING START
The stance a runner uses at the start of a race when their hands are in contact with the ground.

CUE STICK
The equipment used to strike a ball during a snooker, pool or billiards game.

dB (DECIBELS)
The units used to measure how loud a sound is.

DELIVERY
The term used to describe when a ball is bowled at a batsman during a game of cricket.

DRAGSTER
A type of racing car that is used to race along straight racing tracks, known as drag strips.

FREESTYLE
A freestyle contest allows competitors to use any technique they like, for example in swimming, any stroke can be used.

INSHORE
Used to describe something that is very close to the shoreline.

MARATHON
A term used to describe something that goes on for a long time. In athletics, it is a long running race, held over 42 km, usually along roads and streets.

MARTIAL ARTS
Used to describe a method of fighting, such as boxing, karate or judo.

OFFSHORE
Used to describe something that is happening out to sea and far from the shoreline.

OPEN-WHEEL RACING CAR
A type of racing car where the wheels are outside the main body of the car.

PARALYMPIAN
Someone who takes part in the Paralympic Games, a multi-sport event for athletes with a range of disabilities.

PITCH
The term used to describe when a ball is thrown at a batter during a game of baseball.

PROCLAMATION
A public announcement that is usually about something important and made by someone in power.

RINK
The name of a large area that is covered with ice where people can skate and play ice hockey.

ROUNDS
The name given to periods during a boxing match when the boxers actually fight. Rounds usually last for three minutes each, with a rest in-between.

SERVE
The name given to the first hit in a racket sport rally.

SHUTTLECOCK
The object that is hit across the net in a game of badminton. It has a rounded rubber tip with real or artificial feathers behind it.

SMASH
In a racket sport, this term describes when a player hits the ball or shuttlecock with an overarm motion to produce as much power and speed as possible.

STANDING START
The stance a runner uses at the start of a race when they are standing almost upright.

TEST MATCH
Used to describe a match in rugby or cricket that is held between two countries. Cricket test matches can last for up to five days.

VERTEBRAE
The small circular bones that make up the spinal column in a mammal, such as a human.

WEST INDIES
A region of the North Atlantic Ocean, in the Caribbean, that includes many island countries and the waters around them.

WINGSUIT
A special type of suit that is used in skydiving. It has flaps of material between the arms and legs to slow down the skydiver's fall.

INDEX